D1523332

Exploring Ancient

CHINA

with Elaine Landau

Enslow Elementary

an imprint of

Enslow Publishers, Inc.

40 Industrial Road   PO Box 38
Box 398   Aldershot
Berkeley Heights, NJ 07922   Hants GU12 6BP
USA   UK

http://www.enslow.com

"This series tells the stories of the Egyptians, Greeks, Romans, Chinese, Vikings, and Aztecs with texts and illustrations designed to appeal to a broad spectrum of students. While not refraining from acknowledging injustice, hardship, and even the brutality of pre-modern civilizations, the series nonetheless succeeds in presenting these six ancient peoples in a dignified, praiseworthy, and even exemplary light. Highly recommended."

—Nicholas F. Jones, Professor of Classics, University of Pittsburgh

Enslow Elementary, an imprint of Enslow Publishers, Inc.

Enslow Elementary® is a registered trademark of Enslow Publishers, Inc.

Library of Congress Cataloging-in-Publication Data:

Landau, Elaine.
    Exploring ancient China with Elaine Landau / Elaine Landau.
       p. cm. — (Exploring ancient civilization with Elaine Landau)
    Includes bibliographical references and index.
    ISBN 0-7660-2338-9
    1. China—Civilization—221 B.C.–960 A.D.—Juvenile literature. I. Title.
    DS747.42.L36 2005
    931—dc22

                       2004028112

Printed in the United States of America

10 9 8 7 6 5 4 3 2 1

To Our Readers: We have done our best to make sure all Internet addresses in this book were active and appropriate when we went to press. However, the author and the publisher have no control over and assume no liability for the material available on those Internet sites or on other Web sites they may link to. Any comments or suggestions can be sent by e-mail to comments@enslow.com or to the address on the back cover.

All illustrations of Elaine and Max are © Dave Pavelonis unless otherwise noted.

Illustration Credits: © AAAC / Topham / The Image Works, pp. 12 (bottom), 14; © Associated Press, AP / Chien-min Chung, Stringer, p. 21; © Associated Press, AP / Greg Baker, Staff, p. 17; © Bill Bachmann / The Image Works CBAC3159, p. 9; © 2003 Charles Walker / Topfoto / The Image Works, p. 15 (Statue); © Clipart.com, pp. 13 (bottom), 15 (bottom), 25 (bottom), 26 (middle, right), 31 (top), 38 (Emperor); © Corel Corporation, pp. i, ii, 5, 6, 7, 8, 11, 16 (bottom), 19 (top), 24, 26 (top), 27, 38 (Military Leader), 40, 44 (bottom), 45; Courtesy of Government Printing Office, Republic of China, p. 29 (top); © Enslow Publishers, Inc., pp. 4-5 (bottom), 32 (bottom); © Hemera Photo Objects, p. 29 (inset); © Panorama Images / The Image Works, pp. 12 (top), 16 (top), 33 (top), 39 (top), 41 (top); © Photos.com, pp. 25 (top), 29 (bottom, main image), 30 (top), 32 (top), 34, 36, 37, 44 (top); © Science Museum, London / HIP / The Image Works, p. 30 (bottom); © SSPL / The Image Works, pp. 23 (top), 28;© The British Museum / HIP / The Image Works, pp. 10, 19 (bottom), 20, 23 (bottom, right), 33 (bottom, right); ©The Museum of East Asian Art / HIP / The Image Works, pp. 13 (top), 34 (top).

Cover Illustration: Gilt bronze striding chimera, late Eastern Han-early Six Dynasties period, China, 3rd century. ©The Museum of East Asian Art / HIP / The Image Works (top, right); Yunnan, China: City tower of Dali. ©Ma Gang / Panorama / The Image Works (main image); Red earthenware bowl, Xun county, Henan province, Eastern Zhou period, 4th-3rd century BC. ©The British Museum / HIP / The Image Works (bottom, right)

Back Cover Illustration Credits: Jade axe, Zhou Dynasty, China, B.C. 909-225

Contents

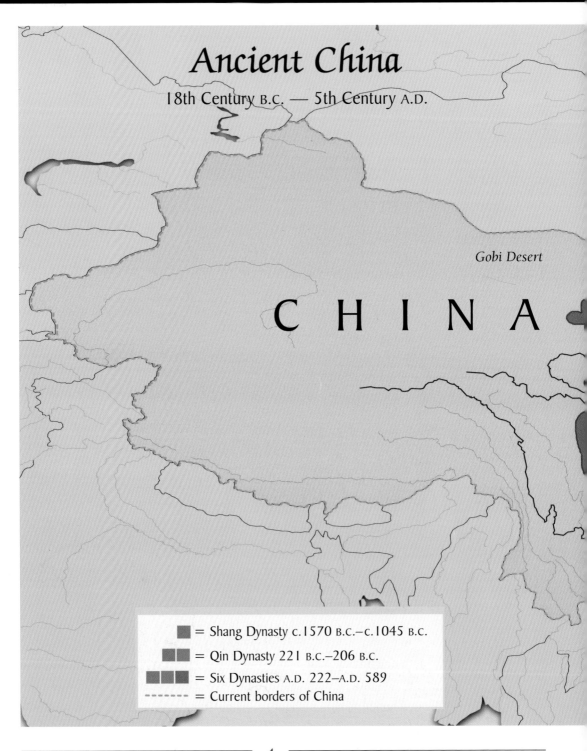

Ancient China

18th Century B.C. — 5th Century A.D.

Gobi Desert

C H I N A

■ = Shang Dynasty c.1570 B.C.–c.1045 B.C.
■■ = Qin Dynasty 221 B.C.–206 B.C.
■■■ = Six Dynasties A.D. 222–A.D. 589
----- = Current borders of China

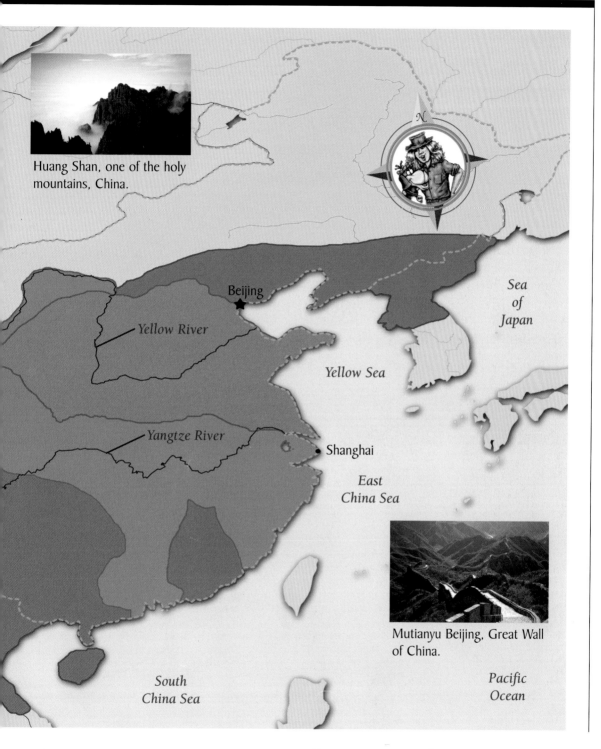

Huang Shan, one of the holy mountains, China.

Beijing

Yellow River

Yangtze River

Shanghai

Sea
of
Japan

Yellow Sea

East
China Sea

South
China Sea

Pacific
Ocean

Mutianyu Beijing, Great Wall of China.

Dear Fellow Explorer,

What if you could travel back in time? Where would you go? You might want to visit an ancient civilization.

I have a special place in mind. The people there invented all sorts of wonderful things. These included the wheelbarrow, matches, fans, kites, and umbrellas. They also invented the compass, paper, gun powder, and a movable type press.

But these people did not just invent things. They were skilled artists and writers. There were also some great philosophers or thinkers among them.

The Jin Shrine was built over 1500 years ago in honor of King Jin.

Spectacular views can be seen from China's Yellow Mountain.

Over time, they developed a splendid civilization. They called their land the Middle Kingdom. They thought of it as the center of the world. We know it as ancient China.

I am Elaine Landau and this is my dog Max. We are about to take a trip back in time. We set the dial on our time machine to about 2000 B.C. We are going to ancient China. The trip was Max's idea. He loves to fly kites and wanted to see the people who created them. Why not join us? Ancient China was a fascinating place. Start your journey now—just turn the page.

IT WAS EASY FOR US TO FIND CHINA BECAUSE THEY INVENTED THE PAPER THIS GUIDEBOOK IS PRINTED ON.

THAT'S TRUE, AND THEY ALSO INVENTED THIS COMPASS.

History and Geography

For a long time, China remained out of contact with much of the world. This was largely due to geography. Ancient China was a very large country with varied physical features. Mountains, deserts, and steep valleys served as natural barriers.

China's climate also differed in various parts of the country. Northern China could be quite cold. Yet parts of the south were very warm—even tropical.

There are hundreds of rivers in China. The two most important are the Yellow River (Huang He) and the

Along with green forests and plains, China also has a wide desert called the Gobi.

The Yangtze is 3,915 miles long. It is the third longest river in the world.

Yangtze River (Chang Jiang). The Yellow River runs for 3,395 miles. It is north of the Yangtze River.

At times the Yellow River would overflow. When this happened, rich fertile soil known as loess was left on the flooded land. People began to settle in this region. They could grow crops in the rich soil.

The Yangtze River is China's longest river. It is thirty-nine hundred miles long. The Yangtze River was vital to the Chinese as well. Ships traveled on it to different parts of the country and the East China Sea. The Yangtze River was used for both transportation and trade.

For many years China was ruled by dynasties. A dynasty is an ongoing line of rulers from the same family. The Xia dynasty ruled from about 2205 to 1570 B.C.

Next came the Shang dynasty. It was in power from about 1570 to 1045 B.C. The Shang rulers were known for their skill in warfare. Sometimes they sent thousands of men into battle. In 1045 B.C. the Zhou dynasty took over and remained in power until 256 B.C.

During the Zhou period, the central government was not as powerful as it had once been. By 481 B.C., much of China had divided into rival regions or states. Though still part of China, these different states were fairly independent. They were run by powerful lords who often fought one another. Each hoped to gain control of more land.

However, things changed in 221 B.C. The northwest state of Qin finally defeated the last of the other warring states. At that point, the different states were united under the Qin dynasty. Shi Huangdi became the first emperor of China. He reestablished a strong central government.

Shi Huangdi took steps to keep China united. Under him, a single system for weights and measures was established. The same was done for money. One Chinese script (form of

Shi Huangdi was the first emperor of China.

The Great Wall of China can even be seen from space.

writing) was now used throughout the nation as well. The first emperor built more connecting roads and canals.

Shi Huangdi was determined to keep the country's enemies out of China. He ordered that a huge wall be built. The wall was largely made by joining together smaller walls that were already there. The wall did not serve as a perfect barrier. A determined enemy could get past it. But it was an important symbol. It warned China's enemies to stay away. The new wall was called the Great Wall. It is the longest structure ever built. Over 4,000 miles long it was built entirely by hand.

WALLS WERE NOT NEW TO CHINA. OFTEN CITIES HAD WALLS AROUND THEM. BEFORE CHINA WAS UNITED, RIVAL STATES BUILT WALLS AT THEIR BORDERS TOO.

WOW, THIS WALL IS HUGE!

The terra-cotta warriors who have been guarding the tomb of Emperor Shi Huandgi were discovered in 1974 by Chinese farmers digging a well.

After the Qin dynasty, the Han dynasty ruled from 206 B.C. to A.D. 220. The Han dynasty also believed in a strong central government. It sent inspectors to different regions. During its time in power, it built a strong army.

Following the fall of the Han dynasty, a new period in ancient China's history began. It is known as the time of the Six Dynasties. The six dynasties were in power from A.D. 222 to 589.

The tomb of Shi Huangdi was recently discovered in Xi'an, China. There, thousands of life size soldiers, perhaps more than seven thousand, stand in formation in three underground pits. They are ready to defend their emperor, whose body lies entombed nearby, from any enemy. They have remained in formation, ready for battle, for over two thousand years.

This bronze figure was made during the Six Dynasties period. The animal shown is make-believe and is called a chimera.

During the Six Dynasties' reign, there was a good deal of war in China. The violence destroyed the unity the country had enjoyed. Nevertheless, important advances were still made in literature, art, and the sciences.

Ancient China was finally reunited by the Sui dynasty. This dynasty ruled from 581 to 618. The Sui dynasty successfully completed the Grand Canal. This is the world's longest man-made canal. It is about twelve hundred miles long.

After the Sui dynasty, other dynasties ruled China. There were also important strides in the arts, sciences, and trade. These served to make ancient China a great power in Asia.

A Jade water container created during the Han dynasty.

Religion

The ancient Chinese accepted different beliefs or religions. Three belief systems or ways of thinking were important in ancient China. These are Confucianism, Taoism, and Buddhism.

Confucianism is not really a religion. It is a philosophy or way of thinking. Confucius was a highly regarded scholar and thinker who was born in 551 B.C.

Confucius designed a code for living or behavior. He said that people should respect one another. He wanted everyone to

YOU KNOW MAX, CONFUCIUS WAS A VERY IMPORTANT THINKER AND TEACHER.

I WISH WE COULD HAVE STUDIED WITH HIM.

This ivory statue shows Confucius holding a scroll. No book definitely written by Confucius exists. His disciples recorded his conversations and sayings in a book call *The Analects.*

treat those around him or her fairly. Confucius believed in the strength of the family. He stressed the importance of a stable society with a strong government.

Taoism is a religion as well as a philosophy. The followers of Taoism disagreed with Confucius. They were against having too many rules of conduct. They did not think that government should be too involved in people's lives. Instead, they wanted people to live as one with nature. Taoism urges people to accept themselves as they are naturally. Striving to get ahead in business or society is thought to be damaging.

Lao-Tzu was the founder of Taoism. He wrote a book that explained his beliefs called the *Tao Te Ching*.

Lao-Tzu holds a scroll with the yin-yang symbol on it. The symbol shows a dark half and a light half. This is to show that there is a balance in nature between opposing forces.

Buddhist monks stand on the steps of a modern-day Buddhist temple.

Buddhism is a religion that began in India and spread to China. Buddhists follow the teachings of Buddha who was born in about 563 B.C. He believed that things like beautiful homes and costly clothes did not matter. Instead, he sought knowledge and happiness.

Buddhists believe in reincarnation. They think that people are reborn over and over. Living as a kind and decent

This giant Buddha statue is in Leshan, China. It is the largest stone sculpture of Buddha in the world.

A Chinese man studies a 1200-year-old sculpture of a Buddha's head in Beijing. The sculpture was recently returned to China after being stolen from the Longmen Grotto in China's Henan province in the early 1990s.

person is important. It means that things will be better for that person in the next life.

Buddhists believe that this cycle of life and rebirth is the cause of suffering. When a person finally learns to live life as he or she should, that individual reaches a state called nirvana. Buddha said that nirvana ended the continuous process of being reborn.

The ancient Chinese never believed that there was just one God. They felt that spirits or gods were all around them. These spirits might be found in rivers, on hillsides, in trees, or even in their homes.

3 Society

C lass was a very real part of ancient Chinese society. Nobles or lords made up the most powerful class. Ancient Chinese rulers gave them large amounts of land. In return, the nobles promised to be loyal. They also fought the rulers' enemies if necessary.

Nobles lived well. Yet the most respected class of people was the country's scholars. They could read and write. They had also studied the teachings of China's great thinkers. Many scholars served as important government officials.

The second most respected class was peasant farmers. They produced food for the nation. The whole country depended on their hard work.

The third most important group was the artisans. These were China's skilled craftsmen. Using precious metals, wood, and other materials, this group made weapons and tools for farming, hunting, and other uses. They also made a

DON'T COUNT ON IT, MAX.

I'VE ALWAYS BEEN A GOOD STUDENT. I PROBABLY COULD HAVE BEEN A LEARNED SCHOLAR IN ANCIENT CHINA.

This rice farmer in China works much like the ancient Chinese did.

variety of pots and containers for cooking and storage. Craftsmen were looked up to because of what they produced. Their items were needed for everyday life in China.

The least respected group in society was the merchant class. Merchants were

This pottery pond was made by a skilled artisan. All kinds of animals are in and around the pond, including fish, frogs, a tortoise, and ducks.

This bowl would have been sold by merchants in the market. It was made in the third century B.C.

often wealthy, but they did not create anything of their own. They became rich buying and selling what others made.

Family life was an important part of ancient Chinese society as well. Chinese households tended to be large. Grandparents lived with their grown children and grandchildren. In most cases, the grandfather was the head of the household.

Marriages in ancient China were arranged by the young couple's parents. A wife went to live with her husband's family when she married. Women in ancient China had few rights. They were expected to obey their husbands. Newlyweds hoped for male children. They sent boys, not girls, to school.

In Chinese homes, respect for elders was stressed. Young couples were expected to look after their aging parents.

Good luck charms like this were often given to a couple on their wedding day.

A young girl prepares to pray during Chinese New Year at a temple fair in Beijing in 2000. The year 2000 was the year of the dragon. In ancient times, emperors thought of themselves as reincarnations of dragons, and children born during the year are considered blessed.

Children were taught the importance of respecting their parents. Everyone was responsible for the family's good name.

Ancestor worship was also encouraged. Ancestors are family members who lived before one's grandparents. In many homes, a special altar was kept to honor dead ancestors. People hoped the spirits of their dead ancestors would guide them so that they would live happy lives.

4 Government

*T*he Han dynasty established an especially strong national government to support itself. It was known as a civil service system and would last for over two thousand years. Those who held government posts were called civil servants. Some civil servants worked on a national level, close to the emperor. Others performed government duties on a local level.

Civil service posts were greatly desired in ancient China. Getting such a post was considered quite an honor. Those who wanted these posts had to take a difficult test. These men usually came from rich and important families.

Much of the civil service test was based on the teachings of Confucius. However, applicants were expected to be good in other areas as well. Sometimes people studied for years for these exams. One emperor even built a university where scholars could study Confucius' teachings.

The ancient Chinese often had to pay taxes. These early Chinese coins were used from 500 B.C. to A.D. 100.

Those with the highest test scores were awarded the civil service positions. Some, who did especially well on the hardest tests, became ministers. These men often worked directly with the emperor.

Other civil servants worked in local districts. They saw that the laws were obeyed. They collected taxes and served as judges. At times, they oversaw road- and canal-building projects. They also made sure that the schools ran properly.

These local civil servants would store away grain in case of famine. They kept count of the people in their districts as well. It was their job to register births and deaths.

Though the civil service system began during the Han dynasty, much later it became the main way to fill government posts in China. Today civil service systems exist in many countries around the world. It is thought to be a fair way to hire people for government jobs.

This type of coin, called a knife coin, is made of bronze. It has an inscription on it which reads "yi dao ping wu qian" meaning "one knife, worth 5000." This particular coin was made in A.D. 7.

The World of Work

*P*easant farmers put in long hours working the land. Often whole families toiled together in the fields.

In northern China, wheat as well as a grain known as millet was grown. Rice was grown in the south of the country. Farmers planted their crops on terraces or narrow areas along hillsides. These high regions had rich fertile soil.

Long rows of rice terraces can be seen in this photo.

Chinese medicine made widespread use of herbs, plants believed to have healing qualities. The Chinese found that some herbs could ease pain, others brought down fevers, and some that treated colds.

The ancient Chinese made sculptures and jewelry from jade.

Yet not everyone farmed. Doctors cared for their patients. They gave them herbs. They also relied on acupuncture, which is still used today. Doctors using this method stick needles below the patient's skin. This relieves pain and helps certain illnesses.

Ancient Chinese potters created decorative ceramic (made from clay) figures. They also made beautiful vases, some from porcelain. Porcelain is a special type of ceramic. Other artisans worked with jade and bronze.

Silk fabric with embroidered scene.

moth

cocoon

silkworm

MAX, DID YOU KNOW THAT SILKWORMS EAT THE LEAVES FROM MULBERRY TREES?

WELL, MAYBE THE WORMS LIKE IT BUT DON'T EVER TRY FEEDING THAT TO A DOG!

According to a Chinese legend, silk was discovered about 2700 B.C. in Emperor Huangdi's garden. Only the Chinese knew how to make silk for 3,000 years.

The Silk Road ran from China into modern-day Pakistan.

They made small statues, jewelry, and other items.

Women in ancient China made beautiful silks. They raised silkworms for this. Thread was spun from the cocoons of silkworms. Then the women wove the thread into cloth. Often they sewed designs into the silk with gold and silver colored thread. Beautiful silks were highly prized in China as well as in other parts of the world. This was because the silks were so smooth and because they were so hard to make.

Merchant traders were often very busy. Many became quite wealthy too. They traded Chinese silk, teas, and spices for horses, wool, fur, gold, and other things of value.

From 140 B.C., they often did their trading along a route known as the Silk Road. The route was called that because traders brought silk from China to Europe along it. The road extended out of China and went through many other countries.

Inventions

*T*he ancient Chinese were great inventors. They often invented items that made their lives easier. Many things we use every day came from China.

Some Chinese inventions were extremely practical. The wheelbarrow was invented by the Chinese in the first century B.C. It was very helpful in farming and construction. People could move loads too heavy to lift.

The compass was also a Chinese invention. The earliest Chinese compass dates back to the fourth century B.C. These instruments would later prove essential to ship captains. The compass allowed them to determine direction.

Still another Chinese invention was important for sea voyages. It was a ship's rudder. Rudders were created in China in the first century A.D. They made it possible to steer large ships. The Chinese built huge ships with very large rudders long before the Europeans did.

Some Chinese inventions greatly advanced their culture.

The Chinese invented the wheelbarrow. This model shows how an ancient wheelbarrow looked

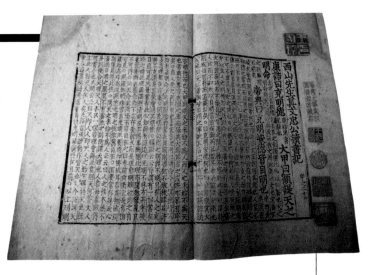

Perhaps the greatest Chinese invention was paper and, with it, printing.

The Chinese invented paper in the second century B.C. Wood-block printing was commonly done on paper by the seventh century A.D. Their first book printed this way was a Buddhist text. It was completed in A.D. 868 By the ninth century, the Chinese had come up with both paper playing cards and paper money. Between A.D. 1041 and 1048, the Chinese invented a movable type press. This later would help

Before the Chinese invented paper money (much like we use today), they mostly used coins.

Kites were used to signal soldiers at a distance.

to make books and other printed materials available to large numbers of people worldwide.

Some ancient Chinese inventions were useful for warfare. Among these was the kite. Kites were created in China in the fourth or fifth centuries B.C. At the time, the kite was not a child's toy. Instead, kites were used by the military for signaling. These kites could stay in the air for two or three days. The military flew them to alert soldiers to danger.

Other ancient Chinese inventions used by the military included gunpowder. This was invented by the ninth century A.D. By the tenth century, Chinese

This model of the ancient Chinese seismograph is decorated with dragons and frogs, just like the original.

stirrup

This sculpture from 649 A.D. shows a soldier with his horse. Look for the stirrup that holds the rider's foot.

armies used flares, bombs, and land mines as well.

The Chinese invented many other things too. By the second century A.D., they had created a seismograph. This instrument showed scientists that an earthquake was occurring. It also showed from what direction the earthquake came.

In the third century A.D., stirrups were invented in China. Stirrups are metal or leather loops that hang from either side of a saddle and hold a rider's foot. Before that, horsemen had to hold on to their horse's mane. Otherwise they risked falling off.

The Chinese made the first practical umbrellas in the fourth century A.D. These were used for protection from both the sun and rain. By the sixth century, lighting a fire became much easier in China. That was when they invented matches.

KITES ARE NO LONGER USED BY SOLDIERS—NOW THEY ARE JUST FUN TO FLY.

YOU CAN SAY THAT AGAIN!

The Arts

The arts were important in ancient China. Calligraphy, the art of beautiful handwriting, was highly valued. Chinese writing is made up of symbols called characters. Each character stands for a word. Ancient Chinese calligraphers practiced for years to form these characters perfectly. Calligraphers were expected to develop an elegant style as well.

Special brushes are used to paint Chinese characters.

Painting was another valued art in ancient China. Many of the painters did landscapes. These frequently featured mountains and water. The artists tried to capture the peace, harmony, and beauty of nature in their work.

Poetry was still another important art. Many ancient Chinese poems praised nature's beauty. Other poems dealt with feelings. Well-educated people in China were expected to be able to write poetry. They were also supposed to develop their skills in calligraphy and painting.

This is the Chinese character for water.

Nature was a very important theme in Chinese art.

Skilled artisans made lovely jewelry, small figures, and other items. Often these were beautifully decorated. The ancient Chinese often worked with lacquer. Lacquer is a liquid coating taken from sumac trees. Ancient Chinese artisans added colors to the lacquer. Then they used it to coat wooden and bamboo spoons, bowls, and other objects. Lacquer adds shine and beauty to items. It also protects them from water and keeps away insects as well.

A lacquer box from the Han dynasty is painted with cloud scrolls and inlaid with silver.

Housing

There were different types of homes in ancient China. Peasant farmers usually lived in mud brick homes. These simple houses were often just one room. They were in the countryside far from the busy crowded cities of ancient China.

This pottery model, made in the third century A.D., depicts a typical Chinese house.

The homes of wealthy families were much bigger and fancier. These homes were often made of wood and had tile roofs. However, it would depend on what building materials were available in the region.

The roofs curved up at the ends. This was said to keep evil spirits from landing on the house. Others claimed that was just how the houses were constructed. No roof was allowed to be higher than that of the emperor's Imperial Palace.

This Chinese house is the type that was reserved for the wealthy Chinese of the time. It has a large yard and the traditional upturned roof.

The Gate of the Heavenly Peace is part of the imperial city and overlooks Tianamen Square in modern China. Above it, the imperial palace rises up.

The large homes of the wealthy were built in sections. Though the sections were connected, there were separate entrances. This was because different generations of the same families lived together. The grandfather and his immediate family lived in the central portion of the home. Close relatives lived in rooms off to the side.

Such homes had an inner courtyard for the family's use. There was also a courtyard outside the home where visitors and merchants stopped. Also, a high outer wall surrounded the entire group of buildings.

9 Food

Most people in ancient China ate simple meals. Rice was an important part of people's diets throughout China, especially in the South. The rice was usually served with vegetables. People in the North ate noodles and pancakes made from wheat. Meat was too costly to have very often. Soybean cakes were their main source of protein instead. Fish was an important source of protein, too.

Food was cut into small pieces. Then it was usually either steamed or cooked briefly in a large iron frying pan. When ready, it was eaten with chopsticks.

Many ancient Chinese dishes were quite tasty. Cooks used different spices for flavoring. They mixed these with various herbs to create sweet and sour tastes. They also relied on honey, soy sauce, ginger, or garlic to make a dish inviting.

Wealthy people in ancient China ate better than peasants. Yet everyone feasted on some important holidays. There were also feasts for weddings and other major events. Special dishes were served at these banquets.

Ginger is often used in Chinese cooking.

However, the banquets of the rich were the most special. At these there were always many different foods to pick from. Besides the different kinds of vegetables, roasted duck, pheasant, and wild boar might be served. Sometimes an unusual dish, such as bear's paws, was brought out.

Bean sprouts

Rice

THE CHINESE USED CHOPSTICKS WHILE MOST PEOPLE IN THE ANCIENT WORLD STILL ATE WITH THEIR FINGERS.

HEY, I FINALLY GOT THE KNACK OF USING THESE.

The Chinese use a simple bowl and chopsticks to eat.

10 Clothing

*P*eople in ancient China dressed in different ways. What one wore showed his or her place in society. Peasants wore long, loose-fitting tops and pants. These were made of hemp and later cotton. Hemp was a coarse durable material made from plant fibers.

Wealthy people and important officials had fancy clothes. These men and women wore long, loose-fitting silk robes. Some of these garments were beautifully embroidered (sewn with designs). People who assisted the emperor wore robes with special patterns on them. This showed their rank. Men wore hats that showed their rank as well.

The Chinese dyed their fabrics different colors.

Emperor

Military Leader

Men wore different styles of hats to show their rank.

Various colors had special meanings. Only emperors wore yellow. White was used to show mourning. It was worn at funerals. The color red stood for joy. Young brides were married in beautiful red silk bridal robes.

Wealthy women in ancient China cared about beauty and tried to look their best. They wore their hair up. It was kept in place with fancy glass, gold, or silver hairpins and combs. Some of the hair ornaments were jeweled. These women wore jewelry and makeup as well.

The Chinese woman in this painting is wearing fine silks.

11 Heading Home

*V*isiting ancient China was terrific. Max adores sight-seeing. He especially enjoyed going to the Grand Canal and the Great Wall of China.

The Chinese accomplished a great deal. Sometimes, the list of things they invented seems endless. We have already seen many of these. But the Chinese also invented fireworks, the mechanical clock, tear gas, the parachute, the suspension bridge, decimal fractions, and an instrument for counting called the abacus. The Chinese discovered that blood circulated through the human body as early as the second century B.C. This was about eight hundred years before the Europeans discovered the same thing.

The Chinese invented fireworks. These fireworks light up the sky over Beijing, China.

Chinese had fans that were often very simply made, but beautifully decorated. They frequently had paintings on them.

Max and I like being out and about. However, now it is time to head home. We are glad that you came on this trip with us. Time travel is always more fun with friends.

To the time machine!

Farewell Fellow Explorer,

I just wanted to take a moment to tell you a little about the real "Max and me." I am a children's book author and Max is a small, fluffy, white dog. I almost named him Marshmallow because of how he looked. However, he seems to think he's human—so only a more dignified name would do. Max also seems to think that he is a large powerful dog. He fearlessly chases after much larger dogs in the neighborhood. Max was thrilled when the artist for this book drew him as a dog several times his size. He felt that someone in the art world had finally captured his true spirit.

In real life, Max is quite a traveler. I have taken him to nearly every state while doing research for different books. We live in Florida so when we go north I have to pack a sweater for him. When we were in Oregon it rained and I was glad I brought his raincoat. None of this gear is necessary when time traveling. My "take-off" spot is the computer station and, as always, Max sits faithfully by my side.

Best Wishes,
Elaine & Max (a small dog with big dreams)

Timeline

c. 2205–c. 1570 B.C.	The Xia dynasty rules.
1570–1045 B.C.	The Shang dynasty rules.
1045–256 B.C.	The Zhou dynasty rules.
563 B.C.	The approximate date of Buddha's birth.
551 B.C.	Confucius is born.
221 B.C.	The Qin dynasty defeats the last of the other warring states and begins to unite China.
206 B.C.–A.D. 220	The Han dynasty rules China; the civil service system is started.
222–280	The Wu dynasty rules.
317–420	The Eastern Jin dynasty rules.
420–479	The Liu Song dynasty rules.
479–502	The Southern Qi dynasty rules.
502–557	The Southern Liang dynasty rules.
557–589	The Southern Chen dynasty rules.
581–618	The Sui dynasty reunites China.

Glossary

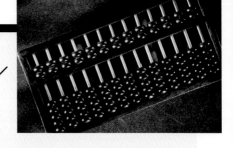

abacus—An instrument for counting.

acupuncture—An ancient Chinese medical process in which needles are inserted at different points through the skin to reduce pain and treat certain illnesses.

ancestor—A family member who lived long ago.

artisan—A skilled craftsperson.

banquet—A large feast for a number of people.

calligraphy—The art of beautiful handwriting.

chopsticks—Narrow sticks used for eating food.

dynasty—An ongoing line of rulers from the same family.

elder—An older person.

emperor—The head of an empire.

famine—A serious lack of food.

garment—An article of clothing.

hemp—A plant whose fibers are used to make cloth.

herb—A plant used as medicine or for flavoring in food.

lacquer—A liquid coating made from sumac trees.

millet—A type of grain.

peasant—Someone who works on a farm.

philosophies—Ways of thinking.

reincarnation—The belief that people are born over and over.

rival—A competitor.

scholar—A learned person.

seismograph—An instrument that shows when earthquakes are about to occur or are occurring.

silk road—An ancient trade route that went from China across Asia and to Europe.

toil—To work hard.

For More Information

Bramwell, Neil D. *Ancient China: A MyReportLinks.com Book.* Berkeley Heights, N.J.: Enslow Publishers, Inc., 2004.

Fisher, Leonard Everett. *The Gods and Goddesses of Ancient China.* New York: Holiday House, 2003.

Freedman, Russell. *Confucius: The Golden Rule.* New York: Scholastic, 2002.

Krasno, Rena and Yeng-Fong Chiang. *Cloud Weavers: Ancient Chinese Legends.* Berkeley, Calif.: Pacific View Press, 2003.

Minnis, Ivan. *You Are in Ancient China.* Chicago: Raintree, 2005.

O'Connor, Jane. *The Emperor's Silent Army: Terracotta Warriors of Ancient China.* New York: Viking, 2002.

Pancella, Peggy. *Qin Shi Huangdi: First Emperor of China.* Chicago: Heinemann Library, 2004.

Wells, Donald. *The Silk Road.* New York: Weigl Publishers, 2004.

Wilkinson, Philip. *Buddhism.* New York: DK Publishing, 2003.

Internet Addresses

Ancient China—The British Museum

Look at all areas of Ancient Chinese life, including a tour of a tomb.

<http://www.ancientchina.co.uk>

Arts of Asia

Visit this guide to art in ancient China. Do not miss the great pictures and maps.

<http://www.artsmia.org>

Select "The Collection." Scroll down and click on "Arts of Asia." Select "Asia," then select "China."

Inventors Assistance League: Chinese Inventions and Discoveries

Find out more about the many things invented in China

<http://www.inventions.org >

Click on "Multi-Cultural Center" on the left. Select "Asian Inventors & Inventions," then select "Chinese Inventions and Discoveries."

Index